FAR OUT
FAIRY TALES

INTRODUCING...

RED RIDING HOOD

PRESIDENT
GRANDMA

PROFESSOR
GRIMM

Raintree is an imprint of Capstone Global Library Limited, a company incorporated in England and Wales having its registered office at 7 Pilgrim Street, London, EC4V 6LB – Registered company number: 6695582

www.raintree.co.uk
myorders@raintree.co.uk

Designed by Hilary Wacholz
Edited by Sean Tulien
Original illustrations © Capstone 2016
Illustrated by Otis Frampton

ISBN 978 1 4747 1026 8 (paperback)
20 19 18 17 16
10 9 8 7 6 5 4 3 2 1

British Library Cataloguing in Publication Data: a full catalogue record for this book is available from the British Library.

Printed in China.

FAR OUT FAIRY TALES

Red Riding Hood, SUPERHERO

A GRAPHIC NOVEL

BY
OTIS FRAMPTON

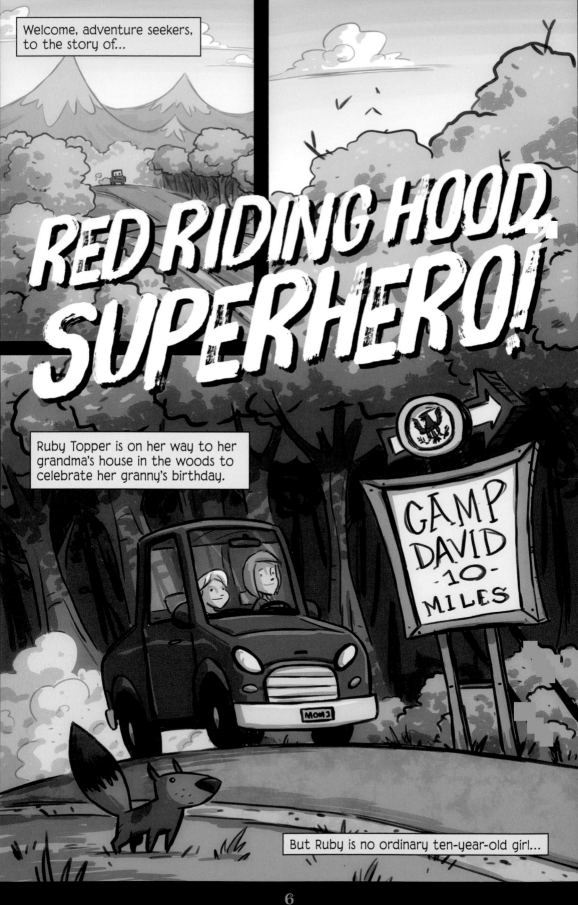

Welcome, adventure seekers, to the story of...

RED RIDING HOOD, SUPERHERO!

Ruby Topper is on her way to her grandma's house in the woods to celebrate her granny's birthday.

CAMP DAVID -10- MILES

MOM 1

But Ruby is no ordinary ten-year-old girl...

And how did Ruby acquire the Red Hood of Power, you ask?

When she was just six years old, Ruby accompanied President Grandma on a tour of Area 54, a mysterious base somewhere in the American south-west.

TOP SECRET
NO ALIENS HERE

While on the tour, she wandered off and got lost in the maze of crates and items that were housed in the facility.

She happened upon a strange creature wearing a red hood and cloak.

!@#$!

You're *adorable!* Let's hug.

The alien, startled by what he thought was some kind of attack, quickly ran away, leaving behind his red hood.

!@#$!

FWIRSHI

Meanwhile, back at the rest stop...

What is taking Ruby so *long*...

FLUSH!

RED RIDING HOOD, SUPERHERO!

ALL ABOUT THE ORIGINAL TALE!

The most popular version
of this particular fairy tale
was published in German by
the Brothers Grimm in the 1800s.
Translated as "Little Red Cap", the
fairy tale tells the story of a young girl who
receives a red cap (or cloak and hood) from her mother.
Her mum then sends Little Red Cap to take food to her poorly
grandmother, warning her not
to stop along the way.

As she travels, a hungry wolf sees the girl walking through the
woods. The wolf asks the girl where she is going, and she tells him. The
wolf suggests that some freshly picked flowers might cheer up her
grandmother, so Little Red Cap stops for a while to collect a bouquet.
The wolf uses the delay to race to her grandmother's house. The wolf
eats Little Red Cap's grandma, puts on her nightcap, and takes her place
in her bed. When Little Red Cap arrives at her grandmother's house, she
gets into bed with the wolf.

The wolf leaps upon the child and eats the girl. A woodcutter (sometimes
referred to as the huntsman) arrives and cuts open the wolf's belly.
He saves the grandmother and the girl, who are still alive in the wolf's
stomach. Then the woodcutter crams stones into the wolf's belly and
drowns the wolf.

In another version of the story, published by Charles Perrault, Red's
encounter with the wolf is a bit different. Red remarks to her
grandmother (the wolf in disguise), "What big arms you have, Granny!"
The wolf responds with, "The better to hug you with, my dear!" The
conversation continues with the child remarking on other body parts
until she notices the wolf's sharp teeth. "What big teeth you have,
Granny!" Red cries. "The better to eat you with, my dear!" the wolf
howls. And the wolf gobbles her all up. The end.

While Perrault's version of the tale ends
badly for Little Red Riding Hood, this
book has a much happier ending.
Take a look at the far out
twists made to this
classic tale...

A **FAR OUT** GUIDE TO
RED RIDING HOOD'S TALE TWISTS!

In some versions of the fairy tale, the red cloak given to Red Riding Hood is supposed to protect her from harm. In this book, it sort of does that too-by giving her superpowers! Red also takes her fate into her own hands instead of relying on a huntsman to save her and grandma.

In the original tales, a woodcutter or huntsman saves Red from the Big Bad Wolf. In this version of the tale, he's a thankful General all too happy to have the superhero Red Riding Hood on his side!

Most versions of Little Red Riding Hood feature a sickly grandmother in need of food and care. In this version, she's the President of the United States!

The Big Bad Wolf is in every version of Red Riding Hood-but this time he's a werewolf! And he wreaks havoc in his Big Bad Wolf-Bot. Only Red Riding Hood, Superhero, has what it takes to stop the menace from kidnapping the President of the United States.

1

Why are these panels coloured differently from the others? If you aren't sure, re-read the story for clues.

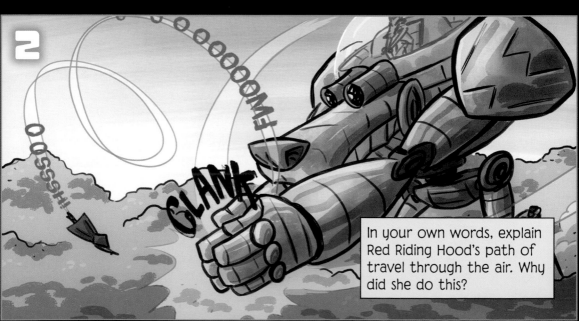

2

In your own words, explain Red Riding Hood's path of travel through the air. Why did she do this?

3

What do the stars over Professor Grimm's head mean? How do you know?

4

OVERHEAT

Red Riding Hood manages to defeat the Big Bad Wolf-Bot by overheating it from the inside. Are there any other ways our superheroine could've defeated Professor Grimm?

GURGLE!

5

Why is Ruby chuckling on page 32? What did her mother say that was funny? Explain your answer.

AUTHOR & ILLUSTRATOR

Otis Frampton is a comic book writer and illustrator. He is also one of the character and background artists on the popular animated web series "How It Should Have Ended". His comic book series *Oddly Normal* was published by Image Comics.

GLOSSARY

accompanied went somewhere with someone, or served as a companion for someone

acquire possess or take control of something

affirmative saying or showing that the answer is "yes"

bladder organ that holds urine after it passes through the kidneys and before it leaves the body

Camp David holiday home of the President of the United States, located in Maryland, USA

domination state of being more powerful or successful than others in a game or competition

impertinent rude and showing a lack of respect

insolent rude, impolite or lacking in respect for other people

ruthless cruel, remorseless or without pity

scheme clever and often dishonest plan to do or get something

sear burn and damage the surface of something with strong and sudden heat

triumph victory or achievement

AWESOMELY EVER AFTER.

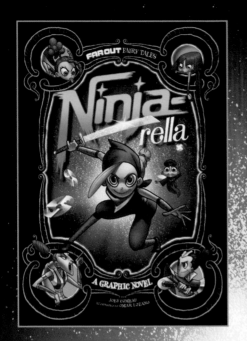

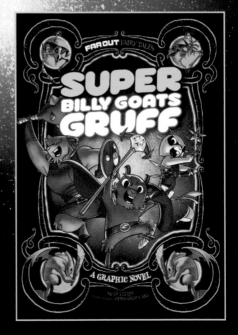

FAR OUT FAIRY TALES